EPIC RITES PRESS

crunked

poetry by Jack Henry

First edition. Printed in Canada.

Editor: Wolfgang Carstens
Interior: Wolfgang Carstens
Exterior: Pablo Vision

ISBN 978-1-926860-01-5

For more information about *Crunked* (and other books and publications from Epic Rites Press) please visit the Epic Rites website at www.epicrites.org, address: Epic Rites Press, 240 – 222 Baseline Road, Suite #206, Sherwood Park, Alberta, T8H 1S8 or contact Wolfgang Carstens at epicritespress@gmail.com.

Epic Rites Press: "because all our fingers are middle ones" ™

some of these poems have appeared previously in different form and i appreciate the publishers of those fine magazines allowing reprint without me telling them beforehand:

tree killer ink
heavy bear
deep tissue magazine
instant pussy
shoots and vines
gloom cupboard

dedicated to those that inspire me:

  Rob Plath
  David McLean
  Felino Soriano
  Mark Walton
  Samantha Ledger
  Tony O'Neill

   &

those that write without fear

   &

Wolfgang Carstens for his constant support

"… I've been reading through *Crunked*, and I'm really, really impressed. You know, I think that you may be the poet laureate of meth culture. I'm not being funny – I think you really captured the surreal and extreme nature of the way of the speed freak, and that the poems veer between being heartbreakingly sad and really, blackly funny. It's really good stuff, very powerful."

Tony O'Neill
author, *Down and Out on Murder Mile*

"Faster, faster, until the thrill of speed overcomes the fear of death!"

Hunter S. Thompson

"The chemistry lesson from last century is that no drug has ever caused as much problems as the attempts to rescue us from them."

Arnold Trebach
Professor Emeritus
American University

Contents

without air he can't scream

he's just a boy –
that's how
the conversation
always starts –

he's just a boy...

doesn't really know
what he's doing
but what he is doing
is something
he should have never known

a small child
...he's just a boy
locked in the last row
of a classroom,
a sort of
permanent exile,
convicted
in absentia
of a crime
not yet named –

his blue eyes
search the eyes of others
but they see no farther
than the end of a nose –

at recess he sits
at the end of a wooden bench
and watches
other boys play football –
girls sitting in clutches

filling the air with giggles
and a mystery he will never solve –

Sister Grace watches,
worries –
never asks questions,
never inquires
from fear
and truth –

from fear and truth
the young boy regresses,
dreams of killing his brother
with a switchblade knife

he has no formation,
no beginning –
all middle, no end –
he runs with the wicked
but never knows sin –

perception to reality

1.

first person to call him
faggot:
      Father – forty-two,
      Jack – only nine

the boy looks into his gray eyes,
   shrugs,
   indifference complete
immune to meaning – Jack (and his friends)
use that word
faggot
   a thousand others
every day –
it means nothing,
just a word,
as innocent as
love
or spaghetti
or...
hey man,
let's play baseball

how do you know anything at nine?

on occasion
Jack uses other terms
other terms he heard his father say
in a joke
or
laughing with friends

on occasion,

Jack got his ass kicked:
>
>
>Saturday morning
>shooting hoops
>on a playground
>– Jack and Joey Littleton –
>Jack calls Joey
>nigger,
>(immunity granted
>from meaning),
>just as he heard his father say
>in a joke or
>laughing with friends

to Jack just a word,
like curfew or spinach
or...
hey man, i love you

Saturday morning
shooting hoops
on a playground
Jack said it, that word, the "N" word,
in front of three older boys
of African-American descent

Jack used to say cunt
as often as he said
  fuck
  or shit
  or some related sanctimonious curse –
Mother put an end to that

in those days
parents cheered
when a child got the belt or fist –
Mother had a good right hook

quick as a spark

2.

Jack grew up
in a mostly white,
semi-affluent
middle American neighborhood –
filled with new cars;
perfumed housewives;
secrets and lies;
and deafening pride

by seventh grade, he learned manners,
if only for appearances –

puberty hit hard and fast –
pure amphetamine
intravenously fed
an endless supply

balls drop,
hair grows thick –
Jack can no longer blame
thoughtless commentary
on youthful ignorance

he became aware

during summer
long and hot
between junior and senior years,
awareness became discovery
and everything changed

everything

made
  sense

3.

Jack rides
an old bike
to a bedraggled strip mall store
in Santa Ana, California
to make a purchase
where anything could be purchased –
  cash up front
  no receipt
  no questions
  no returns

he pilfers
from a meager college fund,
works
twenty hours a week after school
at Safeway
bagging groceries for stay-at-home moms
and pedophiles
snatches twenties from Father's fat wallet
after the old man loads up on cheap beer –

Jack queues up like the rest:
      stiffs
      lemmings
      a rare regular customer with
           rare normal purchases

behind a partition
out of sight
he trades crumpled dollars for crank
    speed

methamphetamine

no one cares,
or asks,
or wonders
it is
a warm April Friday,
three months before
high school graduation,
the man behind the counter –
 a man Jack knows
        in passing
 a man Jack calls
        Doctor
 a man with a beautiful face
   and a strange European accent
offers a deep discount
in the boy's weekly purchase plan –

Jack knows enough
from locker room chatter
gossip in halls
        certain acts –
        the kind of acts
Mother said would send a boy to hell –
        the kind of acts
that makes a father call his son
        faggot –

Jack follows
the Doctor
past a glass case
displaying random wares
for legitimate purchase
to a small room,
that stinks of shit and jasmine,

the Doctor folds a glassine bag
fat with crystal
into a youthful sweating hand

Jack hits three fat lines
lips move
smile out ornate instructions
pants unzip

Jack complies without comment
or hesitation

it seems his father's presumption
became Jack's reality

novice

i'm new at this
i don't know the rules
codes or secret handshakes
if they held orientation
no one sent an email invitation

i know the right street
where to stand
act like everything's cool
as if nothing significant is happening
i try not to be afraid
i try not to flinch at each sudden sound

money changes hands
it's pretty simple
don't talk too much
never ask questions
it's just a transaction

two bindles sit atop my old wood desk,
next to a retirement clock,
a "you're the best dad" coffee cup
a cell phone that no longer rings

i transfer contents
from a button bag
to ceramic bowl
smash rock to powder
cut two lines
roll a twenty-dollar bill

when i was six or seven
kids would laugh and scream
as we ran around the playground

chasing futures without concern

headlines in the paper
– recession deepens
– cities burn
– wars rage
– children die

e-mail remains empty
no offers of employment
i cut another line,
i am
in denial

dreams ass-fucked and bleeding
two years gone and 20k more in debt
cash in my student loan check
at a quick pay joint
in a low rent strip mall
bury crisp bills in my pocket
and walk up to a place i know
all too well

i learn the clichés of using
slang and catch phrases
how to act in a pinch
how to run without looking

~#~

my mother called today
asked for an update
everything is fine, i said
it's always fine
i circle jobs in the paper
go on-line for applications

cut a line for survival
try to write without lying

a friend of mine called
no specific reason
we talk about the future
i lie with each word
he's married, happy, employed
insured
for a moment, i hate him

but it passes

how did i end up here?

how did i end up here?
down in this death dealing
piss stinking mausoleum

with its faded checkerboard linoleum
hissing fluorescent radiators

how did my tolerance fade so fast?
first scream kills all feeling

the only other white person
shrinks toward the door
her face covered
by surgical mask

my stomach burns
it's not something simple
it's never that easy
dying on a gurney
in a long green hallway

how did we end up here?
bent over, internal bleeding
this hen-house never thins out
my vision narrows

soft voices mix
with those of angels
not meant for heaven,
i know,
but it's been a decent ride

when a dead man
on a gurney

coughs up blood,
remembers breathing,
death turns away
disappointed

i thought i saw him smile
toward me

next at the counter
pay what i cannot pay
i hear a little whistle
and trade whispers with the night

finding

i found freedom
at the center
of a rolled-up
twenty-dollar bill
although sometimes
it's a five or a fifty,
depending on payday and
when rent is due

right now,
we're just dancing
two strangers at a bar mitzvah,
or Polish wedding
one more lonely than the other,
yet the
other seems willing to give

every day i eat oranges,
sometimes ten a day,
i buy them
by the bag
from a dark skinned
Mexican granjero

once a week, sometimes more,
i send up smoke signals and
stop by her office
to make the exchange

at the wooden table in my kitchen,
i work the grinder
then put on good shoes,
sit in suspension
wait for music to begin

when i am high i'm a hero,
no one can touch me,
– no one leaves pepper when i ask for salt
– no one can taste me when i'm in flight flying solo
– no one can see me because i'm not there

when i am high
i put away worry,
i put away Sunday,
live the divine

smile serene
thoughts in proper order
i sit at the computer
listen to a clock tick
watch wind bend branches
planes fly over, land at airports
motorcycles rattle windows
cars bump down asphalt rivers

and in the beginning

a poem always starts in my head
sometimes it's all up there
other times

a wisp of smoke
curling toward an
ambivalent sun

sometimes a poem
offers more questions than answers
an indifferent lover, paid
whether i get hard
or not

sometimes a poem kicks my soul
with steel-toed boots
a diamond drill bit tearing my skull
as breath draws baker's dust
to the marrow of my spine

and when a friend finally asks – why do it?
i don't understand the question

poetry's my main addiction
however, the other one,
the one we don't discuss,
the one that occurs behind locked doors,
purchased from street corners

that's the one
that finally gets it done

a harbor in my heart for the soulless in decline

there's a gray hair at the end of my nose –
sometimes i stare at it in a bathroom mirror,
right after i tie my shoes and unscrew a whiskey bottle

sometimes i stand on the street just before a rainstorm
when life is thick and full of heat,
when dreams became matinées at old theaters

sometimes i drive downtown,
order hot pastrami on wheat
because rye bread reminds me of you –

sometimes i drive up Mulholland, past big homes
with the shiny cars and Mexican maids
named Lupita and gardeners named Pete

i never lived in a big house,
with a garden, a proper garage
and a purpose beyond existing
where i stay, it's just a box
four doors, a roof
and a front door that squeaks
from too much passage

sometimes i sit on a curb
and watch rain rivers
carry cigarette butts to the ocean, where they gather in
wastewater basins
and pretend to keep killing –

sometimes i listen for the banter
of crows and canaries,
for mournful yawns of demons and demagogues –

sometimes i take plane rides
to cities of no purpose,
just stand at a ticket counter,
next flight out
sometimes
i talk to others –
a tall woman in tight jeans
stands in front of me
we wait on a restroom –
her smile is in Portuguese,
i translate to Greek

there's a panther in the playground
as the blue pill
dissolves
there's a harbor in my heart
for the soulless in decline

discovery and departure

etched into the concrete floor
of a Greyhound bus terminal,
i found my name carved thick
from knife or fork

my fingers trace carved letters
edges sharp, grooves deep
no one watches me as i kneel to the floor
my East-facing prayer

terminal fills with transients, ex-cons and drug dealers,
it's almost three p.m.

names are listed on a big board
cities and towns
departure times, times of arrival,
some names you recognize, most you cannot

a man of thick beard, untied shoes,
and puzzled stare
looks at the big board, then down at me
he asks: where are you going?
i say: it depends on the time of day
his smile content as he wanders away

destinations mean little
especially in a bus terminal
where i pay in cash
check the time and
depart without further consideration

a house in suburbia

i went to see a friend
out in Riverside
three hours out
on Highway 91
stop and bump the whole way

he has
    a big house,
    a wife,
    a couple of kids
and all related things
one acquires
just to keep up

we talk
a bit

he gets a text message
his mood changes
c'mon, he says,
i follow him to his truck

we drive a maze
of neighborhood roads,
pull onto the front driveway
of a house
not unlike his own

she lets us in,
eyes me with suspicion,
we sit on an overstuffed couch
she offers lemonade,
her ass wrapped in a tight skirt
my friend pulls four hundred bucks from his pocket

puts it into a square wooden box
she returns with glasses of lemonade
sets one in front of me, he gets one too

she sets a small package
wrapped in brown paper
and an elegant bow
at his fingertips
he snatches it up
we leave without drinking lemonade

not a word, he says
but i already know

fifteen points without a center

1.

i am a saint on bloodied knee,
awaiting the church door to open –
my penance is in the waiting
but i am not a saint,
quite far from that reality,
although i suppose there are circles
in which i qualify for something –
a rank, perhaps –
a level of some renown –
if i do, would someone telephone me
to let me know

2.

i am in limbo
        waiting
knees bloodied
        waiting
text message reciprocation
        waiting
trees whipped in mid-winter wind
        waiting
fog filled forests burn down
        waiting
symbols and logic defined in black books
        waiting
pay up and move on

3.

i didn't ask her name
you don't do that

it's against the rules
the ones posted on-line
the ones you need a password for

pay up
move on

she smiles and responds
correctly
without looking away
or blinking

i make passage

4.

holed up in my office
my adventure near its end
like a period on a sentence
no comma or semi-colon
just an end

a fragrance dissipates
without a breeze to carry it

5.

you laughed when i asked for a receipt
tax purposes, you see,
at the end of the year

this is a write off, of sorts
my accountant says this is
research

i hear sirens but the black outside

remains unchanged and a scent of jasmine
lingers

6.

the world seems to stop
just as the second hand begins
to move from one instant
to the next

and i hover over Los Angeles
watching diamonds move down
freeways, sirens blare

little children hear laughter
and look up to watch planes
fly by

7.

at the airport, we collect our bags
cabs stop at the curb
a policeman says move on

a child laughs
mother clutches tiny hand
people speak Chinese

i answer my cell phone

8.

a yellow cab stops
at the curb and a brown skinned
man pulls bags
from an open truck

i tip my cap and pay the fare
you say hello

9.

a man and woman sit naked inside
a bedroom snorting methamphetamine
through one hundred dollar tubes
it is almost morning in Sydney, Australia
a farmer looks to the sky
and sees both sun and moon

10.

a prostitute stands on the corner, once made
famous in movies and forensic science
documentaries on the
Discovery Channel
young and pretty, she is asking for dates

an old priest pulls up,
looks to save her soul
but falls for her smile
and wonders if she can save him

11.

in West Hollywood
two men meet
in the bathroom
of a black-walled dance club
the music is very loud
and it is well past midnight

the two men fumble at belt buckles and zippers

i piss
in a urinal
and listen to murmurs
god's name invoked several times

a nervous man with thin fingers
and gray eyes makes an inquiry

i realize he is not talking to me

12.

in late 2007
i took a shit
in the same
bathroom stall
George Michael masturbated / was arrested in
for lewd and lascivious behavior

i would have done the same
but there were too many Japanese tourists
and i didn't have my rosary beads

there's a park in my old neighborhood
with a similar bathroom
i used to go there to score crank

sometimes i think of George Michael
back when he was in Wham

but there's no irony that i knew he was gay before he
did

13.

two nuns walk past my window

i watch them pass
with mute fascination

one seems to be quite old,
the other
close to my age and semi-attractive

i picture the younger one
sucking my cock
and cranking with me
in my squalor apartment
after i promise to accept Christ
as my personal savior

when my television program comes
out of commercial,
i close my curtains

14.

an old man convicted
of killing five prostitutes
in 1987 now sits alone on death row
in a prison called San Quentin
during the trial he said
god made me do it
i am just a messenger
my acts cleanse the earth of filth

you know, i believe him

according to history, god asked others
to commit unspeakable atrocities
to kill five or more

i believe that as well

when god speaks to me,
i choose not to listen

with every good thing offered,
something bad is bound to appear

15.

inspiration comes from different places
i find mine in the gutter
the old adage is to write what you know

so i do

forgive me father my sins

the same thing
is on television
tonight
as any other
i wait for something to happen
only the clock moves forward

i am anxious
for a messenger
to send news from the front
  a notice of approval
  an announcement that says:
  open until you get here
and i will find freedom
when i get there

i thought the twitch
would switch off
over time
but time burdens me
memory acid etched into
deep furrows
at the center of
my black blood brain,
etched deep with
diamond-tip drill points,

proclamation arrives
via carrier
        come over, i have product
        a little something
        to cut the edge down
        to a manageable burn
        as a part of the deal

          your cock needs service
funny how that
codicil always shows up

~#~

i got high / fucked
first time / same day
thirteen years old
seventh grade, i think
  same circumstance
  same positions
bent over the edge
of an old brown couch
  his cock,
         my ass
  his drug,
         my nose, lungs, and veins

with each fuck i got more dope
with each bump, i want more

eventually
everything becomes equal
and
everything bleeds
into everything else

his cock,
his drug,

my need
never leaves

~#~

i flip through channels
prepare for the street
the box under the freeway
sucking cock for currency

 i never thought i'd be an addict
 i never thought i'd fail completely
 i never thought i'd sit mute and wait
   in front of a television

i never thought i'd know hate so well

crunked

speed doesn't do
everything
i hoped it would

it doesn't
pay bills
or mop floors
or bring me flowers when
        i vomit on the couch

it makes my dick susceptible
        to changing weather conditions
what good is fucking,
        if you can't make it to the end?

out of the gate, i knew the need would build
would become more become more
become more
but i'm not there yet

speed makes my mind nimble
makes me breathe as if content
before i fuck away tomorrow

        you know she is a whore
        when she only fucks
        for money

day becomes night
becomes day before another
and i risk it all
when i taste another bump

i'm not yet a slave

and too scared
to become true reckless

yet i will continue
my illustrious affair

my pathos dance lingers
well after the band refuses
to play on

paths know no direction

it starts with a title
not by design
simple words
a progression
a development of senses
an explosion of light
burning fire
seeing through nucleoli
red blood cells dance beneath
chemically burned eyes

atoms split and split
split down fine white
white hours spin
spinning wheel light
light fires skin
skin aches brittle bone
bone marches against memory
memory crumples against teeth
teeth grind and grind and grind

it starts with a title
chased by verb and noun
built into context
structure and design
collapses on weight
limited in meaning
tap-tap tapping
fingers move
bounce through frames
networks of synapses
lit across my brain

words plummet and fall

fall against blue water
water fills my glass
glass breaks brick
brick builds castles
castles fall with simple words
words are forests of fevered lies
lies dream atop dead leaf paths
paths know no direction

simple truth

1.

a plain, unpainted wooden box
sits unassuming
on a top shelf of a cheap
desk we bought at Walmart
and put together
with a Phillips head screw driver
and a borrowed hammer

2.

some mornings i find Christmas,
a good Christmas
the Christmas where Santa is still real,
kids got new toys,
more toys than used clothes
the Christmas with
a fresh from the box, partially
assembled blue BMX bike
a sober father and a mother not crying –
plentiful dope crushed down to perfection,
a simple touch of a glassine bag
makes your cock twitch

one morning
i found a Federal Marshall
at the door,
thirty days notice
before forfeiture,
time to move on –
father's at the psych ward –
you can't visit,
he doesn't recognize you –

mother explains bi-polar addiction,
affairs with other women,
women you've
met but you keep that
in your mouth –

>there's no dope in the wooden box,
>you can't face
>sunshine or singing finches,
>or a nine year-old
>daughter who looks up so proudly

yeah, that's my dad – did i mention he's a writer?
he wrote a book of poetry for me, my name's in
the title –

3.

the first time i hit a line off silver reflection
in a back bedroom (neighbor's house / New Year's Eve)

i became Superman and i thought:

>it doesn't get better than this

some say an addict seeks the glory of that first kiss
i disagree
i've tasted that same glory time and again,
what i seek now is extension
see how far i can get

4.

we used to make fun
of tweakers in trailers
out in the high desert
bad teeth

wife beater t-shirts,
old rusted Pontiac blocks
pit bulls roaming
trash littered yard
i no longer laugh
or joke
not with a .45 loaded
on the front seat of
my Chevy pick-up

at twilight
(it's always twilight
for some reason)
i wait for a signal,
to make my connection,
and complete a transaction,

like Obama bailing out
Goldman Sachs or General Motors
i stimulate my economy
in a way that i know

the dust of a hundred miles

i'll never be an astronaut
i am more archaeologist
solitude of nightingales
a comfort i prefer

trees outside windows
reference peaceful dreaming
doctors sign prescriptions
soccer moms get high

a girl named Amber Willing
lives silent determination
works every corner
from six a.m. 'til half past noon

i play in stone-edged gardens
with crackheads and vagrant stoners
i struggle with amphetamine
a dance i won't stop

we work though kinks and phrases
burned out alabaster
cut corners toward salvation
with every passing light

Joey knows the answer
Old Otis on the back lot
he has a reputation
a somber kind of skill

we steal from Sunday morning
crumpled bills in our pockets
we pay through secret signals
breathe in amber day

i'll never dance with St. Peter
there's a tweaker in the corner
he's slamming to a backbeat
some day that will be me

for now, i'm a scholar
far from starting over
i passed all my finals
a hero on the rise

i found home in gray fog
up near Easter Island
we lay in fields of rusting
tin cans and copper pennies

don't look at me in wonder
my station here is frozen
in my head i'll be dreaming
in truth i am a clown

digging ditches in Australia
writing poems in arboretums
i know i am an addict
it's not my only vice

last Thursday night

this is not a poem, you see, i cannot write one,
at least, within your expectations –

my kidney is infected, so is my breathing
some kind of germ has taken root –

at the hospital, they gave me antibiotics after asking me
questions about symptoms – there are so many, i said
the nurse did not understand – neither did you –

you see, a poem starts somewhere
goes somewhere
does something
for someone –

however, i don't write like that
so as you said, i cannot write a poem –

they left me in the waiting room with single moms and
families from El Salvador –
i take a hit in the restroom to settle my nerves –
they call my name so i can pay with a credit card
dangerously close to its high limit –

in my head, i see words form line after line –
when they come out i place them on a flat surface
cut the rocks down to powder with the hard edge of a
credit card forming lines on a flat surface
(how many lines make a stanza?)
i roll my last five-dollar bill into a tube and snort
each line back into my skull
rework the poem
in my brain –

it's cold outside as i walk to my car
i have a prescription in my hand
it takes twenty minutes at the pharmacy
i get home
no one is there
you left before i started –

my poem begins with a thought
and forms on a page –

i am tired
i take my medicine
and go to bed –

this is how it works

you go on-line,
create a profile,
upload a picture,
preferably nude,
preferably hard

sometimes it's quick,
some days longer
a hit comes with abbreviations
code that you know

PNP equals crystal, meaning party
fucking high and unprotected

you show up, small talk,
slight confirmation,
he offers you favors,
this is how it works

depending on passion
it might start with kissing
you work your way down
suck on his cock

more dope
more vein blood fire
he fucks your ass
no concern for anything

except the next high

passing fancy

a noise outside my window
awakens me
but not from fear or fright
curiosity rather

my door opens slowly
as my feet slide across
wooden floors
my narrowing focus
eyes a crow in black trees

a bright, full sun is
eager to expose my fleshy excess
but my skin folds tight
over ancient bones

  bones so tired
  bones so weak
  bones that threaten to fall to dust

woodpeckers
play out a chorus
dots-dashes on the thick bark
of a coral tree
koi snap at mosquitoes
that lay in wait on water's edge
silence envelops
what's left of me

i sit on my step
and wonder
at this display of life
and lust
full blooms

and dazzling displays
of radiant splendor
and the first cold rain of winter
begins to stammer against
a brick walk

birds fade,
flowers fold
and i smile,
knowing too well,
that all good things
soon shall pass

freakshow.com

after posting my work qualifications
on six job-sites
after sending out two hundred thirty-seven resumes
for jobs i won't get
after talking to eighty-three headhunters

about commission sales jobs
in insurance, financial marketing,
health care systems
and products that just sell themselves,

i threw in the towel

the state put me on the dole,
sent me a check,
made me fill out the same form
six different times,
a man from unemployment said
a loophole offered me an exemption
some kind of waiver
turns out getting my Master's pays
me $313.54 a week

he said it's a career change into a necessary industry –
his words not mine
perhaps he hasn't read the news about
no experience, no job

i didn't question his good intentions

at my new bank,
(actually my old bank that got sold three different
times)
i cashed

the state check down to tens and twenties
i stopped by my dealer,
he offered me a bargain
a local stimulus package
twenty percent off if i buy larger volume

at a local grocery store
with fluorescent lights
and checkers that act as if they know me
i buy a liter of mid-grade whiskey
i call my bookie
drop the last of my disbursement
on a horse, Sweet Jeremiah at
thirty to one

doped up and drinking
i watch as i win it
bookie pays me my fifties after
a couple of days

i replace $313.54 to my bank account
buy a grocery store gift card
purchase a turnkey adult website
masturbate in the kitchen
crush rocks down to powder
watch the two a.m. news

itch

every day i fight this
craving
this burning itch
that starts at the tips
of my fingers and races
through my balls

why do i stand still
when i need to fly?

my ex-wife thinks i am
bipolar, or
in the midst of midlife crisis

maybe i just found my center
and she cannot exist near the core
or,
perhaps,
i finally eluded
shackles fastened in place
and locked too tight
by matrimonial key

i tried to replace staples
but lost memory pages

it seems my life evolves,
like a poem
not a marshmallow academic one,
nor those written
by rebels and
rabble rousers

more like a poem

built from bottle
or spike, or meticulous sorrow
one that wanders without purpose
or function
a priest at the pulpit
a whore in the grave

tails hasn't come up yet

i am going back
to the real world
one labeled as such
by those that seem to know

it's my revocation
my rapture
crack pipe epiphany

i no longer think,
or study,
or write critical analysis of poets
that shouldn't be alive;
no lectures on surrealism,
or discourse about Ezra Pound,
no circle jerk sittings with
students still unaware

no suffering the sorrow
of Freshman and compositions;
no committees to nowhere;
or fresh bait recruitment

no more writing,
or reading,
or creating out of hangovers;
no portfolio of publication,
reviews or blurbs; no panty-free
co-eds with a superfluous view

now i have so much
they call it a real life
i live by the balls
from seven to six

my dealer's on speed dial,
his product not optional
booze at lunch, always with dinner
travel to Wyoming
that's a helluva ride
with masses in buses
with lemmings on freeways
meetings at C-level and a little below

four nights a road warrior
budget motels and truck stops
slow lanes at fast food
and a young woman named Lucille

i fuck her in an alley
behind 7-Eleven,
we smoke crystal meth,
it's all that i've got

she vomits in a toilet
sweats through thin sheets
i'd guide her to heaven but
i'm not yet built that way

customers keep moaning about
things i can't control
they send me their issues
twenty-four hours a day

managers bitch about projections
wives fuck their gardeners
executives know little
but act like George Clooney

admin assistants suck old cock
from fear of job loss

my fortune is traffic and
electronic voices

they all make predictions
they all get it wrong

my girlfriend left me
house remains empty
my daughter is older
i'm not needed by her now

friends abandoned
my puny tribulations
when i weigh my scale
this is what i've got:

internet masturbation
white line inhalation
one round in the chamber
and the distance to watch

cock tip

cock tip turns purple
when i'm fucking a libretto

from life's communicable disease
we will never wake up

hail to the chief plays on
fallacy transmissions

mourners line alleyways
when high priests tumble by

you called me tweaker faggot
forgot all of your passion

i called you forgettable
with a sinister sneer

we live in the hallows
of oak tree top mornings

we reach out for comfort
yet are swallowed by air

in the back of a closet with forgotten shoes

in the back of a closet
deep in corners, buried in dust,
mixed with sorrowful spider webs
and forgotten shoes
staring at white walls
suffering through silence

his words few, fragmented
nothing but lust and momentary need as
he fucked me

his sobriety came and went

filled with his wicked seed
staring through mirrors of consequence and
muffled desperation,
i long for acceptance
but fear a damning light of reality, of significance,
of complication in a delicate frame

promises made, really just
fancy lies in ladies' garments
all lacy and pink

i huddle with myself
in darkness,
wet woolen despair
hangs on my shoulders,
hands tremble as i search for response

he leaves without words,
nothing new expected
i lay alone amidst tangled sheets
my eyes close and i can still

taste him; feel him,
his scent heavy on my flesh
sleep builds through torrents

solace found in a closet filled
with forgotten shoes and old shirts,
odd memories and broken truths,
garbled transmissions from a radiated world

lies keep building just like my lust

checking out

in the thin twilight of morning
i walk alone on busy streets
in search of a whore and enough dope
to last until my breath finally fades

there is rain,
clouds over blue skies,
the café empty
except for a woman i once knew
her eyes say hello
i remember the price
once paid

she touches the edge of my skin
my cell phone rings
he has what i need,
if i have the cash
we agree to meet

upon return
another woman sits in her place
alone
except for plates on tabletops
she whispers something
i do not understand
in language
i do not know

she writes a phone number
on a square napkin
i realize the form
of a proposition
we come to terms and depart
the night is cold

her bed understands its purpose
we join together
mixed with chemicals
and wine,
a need to escape,
depart
a lust to form around verbs, nouns and perpetual sin

we fuck without passion
another days dies,
black night fills window frames
her mother calls
and they talk awhile
i finally dress,
snort down my last line
and return to the sidewalk,
still breathing,
still moving,
sanguine in my decline

future

there's no future for me

not here, not in words
or pages

my lies have caught up with me
captured, hogtied and spit roasted

i close my eyes
and taste it on my lips
smell it
the burn, that sledgehammer kick
the rush,
you know, like fucking for hours
before you cum
you can't believe it's over

more more more

i fumble with the phone
my twitchy fingers won't focus
there's cash in my pocket
tweaker just got paid

it's never like the first time
you'll never see that castle again
no matter how much you chase it,
you can't catch that tail

but until i stroke out
or my heart explodes
i will never stop running

addict

1.

      i am an addict
a liar
a borrower of false anticipation

i deny my own implication
bent to the glory of your rope

2.

      i am a leper
a pilgrim
a corpse lost in a rotting sea

i dance in fire circles
i remember how to breathe

3.

      i am science
solace
lost in sun and sand

when they toll an august church bell
there's nothing left of me

on getting a job

his office is painted in similar shades of beige –
catalog furniture, plaques on the wall, a picture of Cindy
Loo Prom Queen sits on an oak credenza –
there are golf balls stamped with the names
of corporate clients sitting just so in a wooden frame

an administrative assistant in short skirt, high heels,
painted lips, pushed up tits, bleary defeated eyes, angry
hands,
shows me in and leaves me with a false smile to ponder
later when i am close to passing out

his handshake leaves me sickened, he stands there
in his proud suit, with his white smile, a silicone
stare, mannered hair, trembling eyes, manic brain
snaps –
sit down, he says, if you will, he says
and i clench my fists until there is no blood in my hands
no blood in my veins, my heart begins to slow
and the rage begins to grow

we looked you over, he says, passed around your
resume, he says
we like what we see, we have plans you see,
we have budgets and structures, incentives and
programs,
training and blowjobs,
slit wrists and destruction,
bent over boys in the bathrooms,
dealers in conference,
liars and cheats, stealers, false healers, and a product
that sells itself

but wait! there's more!

my eyes roll into the back of my head
until all i see is myself
in that chair, in that office,
with those pictures and plaques,
and i know this will kill me quicker than speed,
or nicotine,
or fucking a crack whore

an hour goes by,
his erection subsides,
i stand,
he stands
we shake hands,
he offers,
i struggle to breathe,
i sign on the line
piss in a cup,
accept the keys,
buy more dope than i should,
cut fat lines with
a corporate American Express card
on a cheap coffee table
at a Hampton Inn
in El Centro, California and smile

at least i'm getting paid

containment

i'm not wrong,
yet i offer no rebuttal,
even when asked by your sainted lips

i am not proud,
i hide in shadows
make payments on heartache
another blast to the skull

i am not rich,
just common, perhaps anonymous,
most likely – forgotten,
that bitter taste is what makes me whole

i am not stopping,
not that i need too –
i function, most days,
except when fingers begin to twitch

i am not staying,
your congress denied me freedom
just say no killed more
than it could have saved

more awake than dying,
i am not dreaming,
i roll my twenty and take position
continue on my way

i am not denying,
a master's hook cuts deep
through flesh and bone

i am not quitting,

when faced with that alternative
i find contentment

living

right here

methamphetamine (pt. 2)

burn
focus
ache
dead still
silence
watch
wait
drift
word pop
grind
hallow
echo
voice
small
taste
lead
swallow
type
type
type

up all night

it's cold outside

it's cold outside
but skies are clear of debris
i can hear the buzz of a freeway

a black veil has fallen down on me
buried me

my fingers ache as i write

when i get rolling, really moving
making progress by miles and not inches,
i fall down

i trip on a minor point from my past
some little thing that grows
manifests
stretches across the field i just ran through

gardeners do their jobs efficiently, quickly
time is money, in and out and gone
next house, next lawn
a whore can appreciate that

i am supposed to be filling out applications,
forms, providing dates, trying, cajole, convince,
hire, i hold no qualification
put me in a place i do not belong

how much money did i spend for worthless paper?

it's cold outside
the sun rises
people send me email
people place me in boxes

there are no jobs
no stimulus
other than that i inhale

breathing is repetitive
just like behavior
some things will never change

dead sack

i didn't see the fall but i
heard the bounce

seems like another day
here in paradise

out of luck / or / spite
(one never knows)
i found the dead sack first

twisted and torn
i covered her in a blanket
i kept in the trunk of my car

as i looked at her face
and saw her dead smile,
death stood by and
gave me a wink

i wonder who will have the luck
to find my dead sack smile
when that day finally comes

dope on a table

a friend offered me
that which i sought
semantics weighed heavy
but a knife cuts quick

what do i seek, i said
we already discussed this, she said
i do not recall, i said
'
of course not

she cut four fat lines
methamphetamine
atop a beaten end table
early seventies garbage dump couture

you are not what i expected, she said
it's your fault for having expectations, i said

she watched me inhale
each line
without pause
or hesitation
i barely offered
to share
i am sure i didn't offer
at all

she had addictions as well
not speed
not like me
not a tweaker
a gutter level addiction
without the heroin glamour

the crack head humor
prescription forgiveness
she never really explained
i didn't ask
i didn't care
she had dope on the table
what else could i need?

wastewater in concrete sewers

between porn
and
cigarettes
i find
time to write

some days it
flows
– shit filled
wastewater in
concrete sewers

other days
it's like trying
to find a viable vein

only to discover
you're already dead.

perish a thought

night stretches across
artifacts of memory
hot flesh touch
syncopates
with the pulse
of fevered blood

she goes through the motions
of routine

eyes meet
linger
glance away
a bus filled
strangers
and odd dodgers
rumbles down streets
named after dead presidents
rotting corpses
dance in the afterlife

there is no "i" in forever
and the silence
it brings

formal indecision

my madness
keeps growing
historic buildings
torn to rubble
dust streets with
old skin
and asbestos

indecision mars my path

at seven
a young boy
plays
on city streets
buried under
blaze light
of Autumn

a panicked classroom
fills with
hopeful tomorrows
even then

i knew

even then i felt
the pulse in my skin
my destination
foretold
the first time
i wandered under
a short pink skirt
on a Hollywood whore

a Hollywood whore
no older than me
no brighter than me
whose dreams
slow turn
from Prince Charming
blowjobs
to heroin and
methamphetamine

my dreams turn too
just as air returns to shattered lungs
just as a parade passes by

she once whispered
in my ear
and i thought
how can i refuse?
but terror filled her eyes
when my smile
began
to show

lines like diamonds or maybe pearls

real unreal
a sky tortured by too much blue
sea gaze dreaming
flowers grow through stone

midnight incantations
words across a page across a wire
through damp breezes that linger just so
atop tall pine and conifer

i tear off my mask
she tears off her pants
i never took a road less traveled
seems i always got lost

your faint hello, a mystery
but reasons never matter
a coiled snake waits in a box
discordant melodies play on a slide trombone

Jim Morrison dances while Sid and Nancy
spit on fallen priests
i used to live in Wisconsin
but California's my home

alone in public

i am sitting
     at
          a wooden table
     on
          a wooden chair
my back hurts
i am restless
it is
     Wednesday
and i should be doing
     more

i cannot focus

Russia is too cold in winter
i had Chicken Kiev for lunch
my stomach is not right

i scored a gram of speed
     a little better
     now
i am

nothing interesting
conversations continue
too many boring people
myself
     included

i just realized
they don't play music
at Border's Bookstore
i could ask but really, who cares?

Kelly Clarkson has become an obsession
i am not sure why
she's a little too proper for my
Satanic rites

there's so much left to be done before retirement
wills to sign, documents to proof, payments to be made

people fill the café
the bookstore becomes crowded
my bed is uncomfortable
spaghetti would be a good dinner
a little basil and butter

and a nice Chianti

no promises left to keep

seeking solace
eyes shut dreaming
demons dance
across my skin

acrid air
cannot breathe
cannot see through clouds thick
and black

cannot see through morning
to a brighter sky
a bright day
clouds keep chasing
chasing
clouds keep...

there's a sound i hear
in the back of my mind
a shotgun blast from
a fading smile

there were days
when i found peace
in soft petal folds
between her legs

there's no peace now

demons dance atop
my flash

a phone call away
money i shouldn't spend

a purchase i cannot afford
the first line hits
and hits
and
          hits
and i drift
          slow
back to where Alice plays

i never dreamt

                    in color
          where
                              baseball
and
                    summer days
filled
          my   eyes
now i lay me
down to sleep
i pray and
                              i pray
and i dream

          of dope and junk
lines neat and orderly
on antique mirror

and now?
and now...

now
it's all i see

that
                    first

                hit
drill bit split
                    my skull
my   reality
                    gone baby
                                    gone
an   d
                    i   c o u l d
            re   all   y

c
a
r
e

less

honesty. really?

did i ask you
or you me
when did this start
i can't recall
anything more
than the conversation i had with god
about the birth of Christ

good times never last
as long as bad
and bad always remain
memory locked and loaded
and yes that dress makes you look fat
try something different
something with stripes
vertical not horizontal
maybe black
maybe just stay home

my mother said, more than once
that i should be nice to people
that i should do onto others as they do onto me
that's irony
right?

when a man in a bar punches me in the eye
(seems i look like his wife's lover)
i help him up when i knock him to the floor
when a mugger attempts to rob me
i apologize for breaking his nose
when a surly cashier at Walmart gives me grief
i smile when i call her a cunt

underneath skies of diminishing returns

welcome back
        she says
in a hazy blue way
welcome
        she says

and i am home

i turn in the keys
after locking the door
one last time

pockets empty
except for one thing
the only thing

i want

wrapped tight
in thin plastic
the plastic you use to cover food
so it will not spoil
the plastic you
find
in sheets
at the grocery store on Main Street

knot tied
almost too tight
undone
contents spill
on cracked tile
carefully i crush
crystalline rock

to powder
        nearly pure
        nearly perfect

lines cut
tube rolled

my heart conspires
my cock stiffens

when i take that first hit
        i cum
when i take that first hit
        i smile
when i take that first hit
        my left eye waters
        my brain burns
                the voices silenced

and i hear nothing
and
        everything
it all makes sense
        now
it all seems
        so clear

until
there is nothing left
nothing wrapped in plastic

until there is nothing

                                left

i'll just call her bitch

how'd i get here?
this place?
this time?
out of money
scratching couches for fallen change
digging streets for scraps of this or that
how did i fall do so fuckin' low?

and don't say it
i'm way ahead of your spinning

yeah, i'm better off than some
yeah, i got a roof most nights
yeah, i eat three square meals some days
but fuck that fuck you
fuck it all
i'm tired
out of dope
out of patience
out of second chances

some say poetry
should uplift
explore
expose
create
uplift my cock
kiss my sweaty balls
yeah, that's where i'm at

maybe you haven't realized
that this ain't art

you look at me

hand out looking for hand outs
twenty here, there, everywhere
banks closed
doors padlocked
sign says bankrupt, fucked up

it's always about
loan me ten
maybe thirty
how about fifty
sad-sack Jack just goes along
to get along

pity party sure
my party
banner on a bedroom wall
piñata hangs from a beam
bat in hand
and i can't bring myself
to slaughter an ass filled with Mexican candy

maybe if i score
maybe if i pass out
maybe if i run away
maybe if i uncock the hammer

maybe if i went balls up
left the soft ass motherfucker
on a corner
where a bus might stop
and take him away
i can regain

even then

and

even then

she'll let the dishes stack
the animals starve
complain
and
complain
and complain

move on move out
fuck off
do something
just something

anything

but don't expect me to say please

when you go
and you will go
be in box under dirt
or
shotgun wedding to a twelve-toothed tweaker
i stand
wave
and never give it another thought

equanimity amongst the living

an old poet
sits on a wooden park bench
feeds pigeons
stale popcorn

he takes small handfuls
from a small brown paper bag
spreads it around
enough for all

enough for all

he awaits
arraignment
prosecuted
for ego
nihilism
and a generally pissy attitude
toward all
except for the pigeons
and
occasional parakeet
that happen by

he tossed away
everything
for a taste
a simple lick
of something
never offered
never available
even at a discounted rate

he once brandished a crown of thorns

stood taller than a Roman cross
touched a sun high above the clouds
of an emperor's sky
and never fell

he never fell

a simple lick
that delicate flavor
etched deep
in his ugly face
a face marred by epiphany
and pursuit endless
consumed
committed

he dare touch the very face of origin
and
lift a sainted skirt

there within
        an embrace everlasting
there within
        a tomb sheltered without stone
there buried
        deep in silk sheets in a third floor
        apartment in Hollywood California
the taxation of reality became
a burden not worth the bear

shuddering in his corner
skin popping veins with twisted needle
searching and searching
for disclosure
simple silence
equanimity amongst the living

a demon amongst devils
fucks him without mercy
or passion
or care

and as he lay in pools of memory
her whisper voice lingers
meaning still tempts him
but her lips no longer move

perhaps if i fucked you

perhaps
i removed the spleen
– too soon
in search for a soul
(perhaps)
a soul revealed
balances less in light
– more in pitch
– more in black
– more in depths of harrowing sorrow

perhaps
i removed the taste
of your skin
from aging memory chips
– too late
a croaking dawn emerges
atop foreclosed houses –
women push baby strollers
while collecting aluminum cans
from trash receptacles in alleys –

perhaps
my new obsession,
a reboot of something familiar,
brings my insanity
– too close
narrow eyes stare at me –
i stand waiting,
cigarette on lip –
smoke curls coils drifts in a dew ridden day –
this wallow is my own choice,
clearly –

perhaps
if i fucked you
(just to fuck)
your cunt would still welcome me
– too bad
streets harbor my bones
in a damp entrance
of businesses
long in disrepair –
i am told the sun still shines
on this side of a callous world,

i wonder

sober eyes

there in the sky
above my house
above my bed
clouds
gather
disagree
and move on

a mid-winter setting sun
paints outside dotted lines
purples and pinks and random blues
cloud cracks reveal
rails of light
heaven's spotlight
on damning sins

little girls
in pink jackets
play softball
and giggle about things
they are not sure of –
father's watch intently
discourage a lone
pedophile
with fists and
baseball bats

soccer moms
purchase groceries
dream of youthful days
watch young men
let the warmth spread
before blushing
i look at her as she looks at them

rain threatens
or so they say
winter rebels against
printed expectations
alone in my wasteland
lines before me
a rolled bill in hand
i prefer the blindness
of amphetamine
to that which sober
eyes see

dance then on the grave of a dearly departed

when did i fall?
when did i fail?

there are those that do not like
the way i write
choices i make
a battle rages
between
verb and vowel

too much sorrow or pity or something
they cannot comprehend
and that's fine
that's
      okay

move along motherfucker
move   along

maybe words
are all i have
maybe lines
are all i know

i never said
i write for you
never said
anything, really
      at all
never spoke about a concept or theory
         or paradigm
there's no discourse between
you and i
and me

and words
lines   on pages
              on glass

a preacher stands at a pulpit
spits his words into air
lets them fall into ears
and
parishioners stare
        wonder
        question
he is lost
they   are lost
they sit together
they wonder   together
they pray   together
and outside oak doors

and outside oak doors
under blue American skies
things   fall apart
dreams   fall apart
lives and loves and harbored hope
        fall apart

preacher has faith
on his knees
has faith
        just as a whore has faith
        the cock in her mouth
        is the last paid cock
        the last cock unwanted
            just as a junkie
            depresses the plunger
            watches a rose bud bloom in the cylinder
            before release

before descent
before that moment

and we all have moments
– in the eyes of our children
– in the smile of a lover
– in success however brief

i should never have been a poet
never went back to school
never placed my future in another person's hands
never asked forgiveness
never reached so high

my wings have melted and now

and now

and now i am falling
back to dying earth
back to bright light clarity

there's a day coming
coming soon
        that day
that long gray day
when i find restitution
of soul and spirit and mind
six feet deep
buried under rock and dirt and stone
you can dance then
return to living
        dance then
on the grave of a dearly departed

i won't mind

                    not really
                    now i know
i gave up
the moment
i drew my first breath
and kissed sweet
the atoms of opportunity

just a moment

they nestle in clutches
by numbers
always even
twos and fours
never three or five
they whisper
make arrangements
exchange currency
for communication
or product
or a back alley fuck

i've already made my provision
there's no need to stop

streets remember
footsteps
just as a Korean grocer
sweeps his front step
pauses to smile
and wave
speaks my name
thick with regret
i wonder
if i owe him money
or if i stole something
of no value

i nod and smile
as a polite thing to do
step to a polished counter
ask for a bottle
his wife, Kim, already knows
Pavlovian manifestation

sad crumpled bills
fall from pockets
she puts the bottle
in a brown paper bag

a small girl
with black hair
and large round eyes
looks up at me
a Barbie doll in her hand
she smiles
her teeth not yet corrected
i say hello
her mother smiles
proud as most parents are
back through the door
i say good day to
the Korean grocer

he continues to sweep
as i walk away

a slow inching forward

chaos sits harbored at the center of my soul
awaiting its exposure to graceful rays of inanimate light
each tick of the second hand on my grandfather's clock
only reminds me of a slow inching forward

burn down your castles, your kingdoms
unhinge doors from bird cages
wrestle free your passion
never bury your sorrow

i drink from a wooden cup
cut from birch trees dead on forest floors
and filled, each day, in renewal

a rope cinches tighter
around my neck, ever forward pulled
i deny your words as they splash
into pools of blackened blood

wrest free from the grasp of Death's thin bones
feet lead me past the galleys of long dead warriors
my eyes no longer rest on your skin
my eyes no longer see past red sunsets

you have left me,
        without verse or voice
you have left me
        stilled in building tides
you have left me
        atop buildings awash in fire
you have left me
        alone

just as i knew you would

heroin hand me downs

heroin hand me downs
linger near windows
shopping for product
they come – two by two

breeders and chasers
gather in clutches
dealing against death
the devil takes his time

i want for connection
last stop redemption
a guy i know as Bobby
makes his approach

five tiny bindles
angels in sunshine
i pay with the rent
techno-bebop plays live

hookers in corsets
wait for acceptance
trade blowjobs for passage
night seems to thrive

my mistress lay waiting
white line simulation
my cock suddenly eager
the clock begins to slow

three days no sleeping
royalty check payoff
i keep throwing snake eyes
and swimming in sin

breakfast at the Pancake House

a chorus of old men
line a counter
i am an old man
                          now
some stare off onto a blank space
on the wall
some read newspapers
filled with:
            bombs in Afghanistan
            1600 county jobs cut
            maximum sentences for dog killers

hey Obama
            heard about Massachusetts
            blue to red
            panic in Democratic War Halls
            Supreme Court changes
            earthquake in Haiti

seems like you're a little busy
seems like more of the same
seems like things down here
                  in the mud
                  on my street
            haven't changed
                          much

arranged my own stimulation
via debt reconciliation
destroyed my credit
            it's fucked already, ya know?

Bush's recession destroyed
            my future

Obama's solution destroyed
        my hope

we keep sticking our heads
        in the sand
too busy struggling
too busy breathing
                i guess

in my pocket i hold my other stimulus package
bought with cash
although my dealer offered credit
but he's too embarrassed to match the rate
        Bank of America charges

got the special, Mr. President
at the Pancake House
$3.29 plus tax
and a side of sourdough

might score another gram
        of dope
i know i shouldn't
you keep spending money
        to stimulate the economy
and i'll do the same
        to stimulate mine

happy birthday to me

i taste her sweat
as my tongue traces circles
from breast to breast
nipple to nipple
she smells of fear
and spontaneous combustion

her smile trembles
as i pull off her panties
her hand unzips my pants
my Viagra kicks in

we have names
but don't share them
lack of proper introduction and
protection of others
she charges by the hour
by now we're old friends
today i get my birthday discount

she offers to kiss me
but i know where that mouth's been

it takes longer than usual
a sweet syncopation
she almost didn't fake it
when size seems to matter
that's where i fail

write me a poem, she says
covered in towels
something sweet i can remember
so i write her this poem
before we hit it again

about Jack Henry

Jack Henry is a writer based in the high desert of SE California and grows increasingly obnoxious and annoying with age.   Recent publications include *with the Patience of Monuments*, on neoPoeisis Press (www.neopoeisispress.com) and *The Downtown Cafe*, on Erbacce Press (www.erbacce-press.com).   He has been fortunate enough to be published in a variety of journals and magazines both in print and electronic. He can be found at jackhenry.wordpress.com if you are that curious and need more.

also from Epic Rites Press

Frostbitten by Mark Walton
A Bellyful Of Anarchy by Rob Plath
Hellbound by David McLean
The Broken And The Damned by Jason Hardung
Dead Reckoning by Todd Moore
Doing Cartwheels On Doomsday Afternoon by John Yamrus
Crudely Mistaken For Life by Wolfgang Carstens
Laughing At Funerals by David McLean
The Epic Rites Journal: Building A Better Bomb
There's A Fist Dunked In Blood Beating In My Chest by Rob Plath
Blood And Greasepaint by Karl Koweski
Can't Stop Now! by John Yamrus
We're No Butchers by Rob Plath

epicrites.org